Dealing with a playboy

Think otherwise and get completely heartbroken

TONY ALBERT

Table of Contents:

Chapter 1

When you become aware that your man may be or is being unfaithful, the life you have created with him comes tumbling down. There may be a lot in your thoughts right now, questions about the past, the future, your relationship, and how uncertain everything is. Countless thoughts may race through your head.

When you're in a relationship, there are many things you look forward to, such as love, hugs, and loyalty, but what happens when you unintentionally end up with a playboy? These days, it's difficult to spot a playboy since they've mastered the art of blending in. They are skilled at manipulating you to get more pleasure. Because playboys are playboys, you'll be nothing more than a score on their scoreboard. We all want to change the playboy or the game, but it's not very feasible considering how unlikely it is that a playboy will leave the field before you become his victim! This is primarily because when we fall in love, we frequently ignore the warning signs and become unaware of all the warning indications we would have considered carefully! Heartbreak is the only possible outcome when dating a playboy. A playboy is all about the game; as a result, he won't commit and will never show you true love or loyalty. Because of this, it's critical to recognize the indicators that indicate your boyfriend is a playboy and has been using you as a pawn all along.

Chapter 2

Indications that your partner is a playboy:

1. He refuses to recognize or acknowledge you in front of others:
Your relationship is kept a secret, similar to how he would keep his dirty laundry from airing out in the open.

2. He guards his phone like a dog guards a bone:
So a player's hub is his phone. It's where he organises all his women and where he keeps contact with things going on so that he can keep them all on the rail.He will do everything possible for you not to come across his contact.

3. He dates far too many women, and he frequently forgets who his intentions were. He probably abandons you so frequently because of this.

4. He jumps into bed with you too quickly: He frequently calls you late at night asking for action because he's always itching for some! You feel less like his girlfriend and more like a booty call when he is with you.

5. He makes plans he doesn't follow through on:
So, unlike a guy that's straight out using you, a player might actually make some future plans, they won't be long term extended future plans but he's likely to tell you what you want to hear and you guys are going to see each other in the next week or two.

6. He can read you like a book; he knows everything about you, even down to your weak spot, but you don't know all about

him. He resembles a riddle you haven't been able to crack.

7. He rarely calls you: A man who is truly in love with you will constantly want to call you at the first chance he gets. When he doesn't hear your voice for a day, he feels an emptiness inside.

Calling you becomes a difficult challenge for a guy who is dating you but is not interested in you since he is a playboy. This is because he is surrounded by other girls who, like you, need his attention.
His only responsibility is to take advantage of you all while misleading you in the name of our relationship. On time, flee for your life.

8. Your connection feels quite surface-level. In comparison to you, he is less involved. He doesn't show any interest in the relationship or take any effort, and you don't go on dates as couples often do! He keeps his emotions

to himself. He appears to be concealing something. He doesn't even appear real or romantically involved.

Perhaps the most challenging of all of them is whether you should simply ignore your cheating man and move on or stay with someone who cheated on you. Even though leaving a cheating partner may be your first instinct, it's not always simple to end a relationship.

However, there is always a solution to any difficulty, and this one is no different. You may convince him to be completely devoted to you.

Chapter 3

Knowing what to avoid

You are not to blame:
Sometimes your partner's motivations for infidelity may not be evident, and you might believe that placing the responsibility on yourself is the only logical course of action. Perhaps you believe that you have been aloof or that you haven't been particularly candid in bed. Perhaps you've let work get the best of you and neglected the relationship.

Nevertheless, while these might be signs that your relationship needs some more effort, you should be aware that nothing you do can ever lead to your partner cheating, and you shouldn't ever hold yourself responsible for your partner's errors. Undoubtedly, you might be to blame for a certain issue in the relationship, and it's

crucial to accept that. However, you must never, ever believe that your error excuses your partner's infidelity.
If you put too much emphasis on taking responsibility for your actions, your partner will be exonerated. You must pay attention to how your partner is acting as well.

Don't obsess over the third party:
Asking a million questions about the other woman, spending hours watching that person's Facebook profile, or even attempting to catch a peek of this person in person are all ways to quickly drive yourself insane. Although you may believe that learning everything there is to know about this person will help you understand why your relationship failed, in actuality, doing so will just make you feel even worse.
Rarely does an affair involving a partner involve a third party. The majority of the time, cheating is essentially a reflection of the cheater's dissatisfaction with himself or

the relationship, unless that partner believes he has truly begun a serious connection with a third party. You won't be considering your partner or the relationship if you place an excessive amount of emphasis on the other woman.

Even while learning a little bit about the affair can comfort you, you might not want to learn too much about the other person's appearance, occupation, or any other characteristics that could distract you or make you feel self-conscious. It simply isn't worth it.

Don't tell everyone:
You can feel wounded and angry and want to tell everyone in your family, your closest friends, or even post about it on social media to fully get your feelings out. Instead, resist the desire. However, if there is a chance that you want to make things right and reconcile, you'll have to put up with

people's perceptions of your partner and your union. Tell only the people close to you who you believe can help you think things through, as opposed to telling everyone you know.

You might have some initial comfort after telling everyone what happened, but that relief might be followed by regret. It's possible that you were unprepared for everyone's opinions or criticism.

If you do decide to inform your close friends about your partner's infidelity, proceed with caution. If your friends believe you're going to break up with your partner, they might list all the 1,000 things they didn't like about him. This won't help you feel better, and it might make things difficult later if you decide to stay.

Don't worry excessively about what people will say or think about you. You should keep

what happened to yourself and not be concerned with what others who know about the affair may think. Although others close to you can offer you helpful advice, ultimately it comes down to what's best for you. If you decide to leave or stay in the relationship, you shouldn't worry about what other people will say.
In the end, it doesn't matter what other people say, and you shouldn't let their opinions influence the choices you make.

Speaking with those who are close to you can undoubtedly provide you with strength and a fresh outlook on your circumstance. But in the end, remember that their views can never take your place of yours.

Do not make significant decisions without thinking:
Even if you might feel the want to leave the relationship as soon as you learn that your boyfriend is cheating on you or packing up your belongings, you need to give this some

more thought. You can spend some time apart from your partner, but hold off on declaring that you want to break up or take any immediate dramatic action. Instead of acting in a way that you might later regret, give yourself time to think about what happened and what is best for you and your relationship.

Even while deciding to spend some time apart right away can be a good thing, you should refrain from declaring that you want to end the relationship. Even though this may be what your mind is telling you to do, wait until you have a clear head before making this final decision.

Don't punish your partner:
Taking away the things they enjoy, or even having an affair in revenge may feel nice but these actions won't go you very far and won't advance your relationship. Even while you can be hurt, distant, and cold to your partner for a while, you shouldn't

purposefully make them feel worse because that will make both of you feel awful.

Punishing your partner will simply make you bitterer and will make you feel worse about your relationship. Being more chilly and aloof than usual while spending some time apart is acceptable, but purposefully being mean won't help the situation.

Chapter 4
Taking a step

Make your demands:
Before you start a talk with your partner, you should spend some time considering what you want from him. Don't just begin by discussing the infidelity before sobbing and making up. Instead, spend some time coming up with a strategy so your partner is aware of what you need from him if you

want the relationship to endure. This shouldn't come off as a punishment, but rather as a strategy for moving forward as a team.

Tell your partner what he needs to do to keep the relationship going. Making time for conversation every night, going to counselling together and potentially separately, taking solid efforts to rediscover the things you loved to do together, or sleeping in different rooms until you feel comfortable sharing a place again are all examples of how to achieve this.

Give it time:
You should be aware that it may take a long time to rebuild the trust and love you previously felt for your partner, even if you are truly ready to forgive him or for things to return to normal. It can take a long time for things to feel, for lack of a better word,

"normal" again and for you to feel fondness for the person you love, even if you two are determined to make it work. This is entirely normal. You could get into trouble if you try to move things ahead too quickly.

You won't be able to instantly feel like things are back to normal or can forgive your partner. Regaining that trust can take months or even years.
You'll also need to move slowly. It can take several days for you to feel secure enough to share a bed once more, go out to dinner with him, or simply enjoy doing the things you used to like doing together. Prepare yourself for that.

Express your emotions:
Inform your lover of your feelings. Tell him about your hurt, rage, betrayal, and pain as a result of his actions. Allow him to truly see and hear your anguish; don't keep your guard up and pretend that it wasn't a huge

problem. You won't ever be able to fully move forward together if you're not upfront and honest about what you're going through. You must express your actual emotions, despite any shyness or fear you may experience.

You can write down everything you want to say if you're worried about speaking in front of your partner or not saying everything you wanted to. In this manner, you can avoid becoming distracted and overlooking a crucial issue. Give it a few days or wait long enough to feel comfortable talking about what happened if you're too emotional to talk about it right away.
Naturally, you might never feel entirely at ease throughout the chat, but if necessary, you can take some time to settle in. So maybe don't put off having this topic for too long.

Ask the queries to which you seek the answers:

Regarding what your unfaithful partner did, you might want more clarification. Asking questions about how frequently it occurred, when it did, how it got started, or even how your partner feels about this other person, will help you piece together how this has been going on. However, you should think twice before inquiring about information that you might be better off not knowing if you want there to be a chance that the connection will endure.

Any inquiries that you believe will give you a better understanding of the status of your connection with him are welcome. However, try to refrain from asking questions only out of curiosity; the responses can prove to be too painful.

Get a medical exam:

As embarrassing as it may sound, you should both be tested as soon as you discover that your partner has cheated on you. You have no way of knowing what illnesses the other person may have had, let alone if they were transmitted to you. Although your partner could argue that it isn't required, you must take this step to ensure your safety as well as theirs.

This procedure will assist your partner in realizing the seriousness of their acts.

It's crucial to realize that sleeping with someone else while they were also sleeping with you puts you in danger.

Pay attention to your partner:

It's crucial to sit and listen to your partner even if you may be feeling upset, overwhelmed, betrayed, furious, and a host of other emotions that you want to express. Although you could feel that listening to him is the last thing you want to do, doing so is necessary if you want to move the relationship forward and gain some clarity.

It's unfair to assume that he doesn't have a right to express himself or his feelings in this situation. Let your partner express himself if you want to move on, even though you may not feel ready to address his feelings.

Daily communication improvement: You can focus on enhancing your communication once you and your partner have started talking about him cheating. Be sure to communicate frequently, be open and honest, and steer clear of passive aggression whenever you can. Even though this could seem difficult given what your partner did, if you want things to improve, you must communicate as effectively as you can.

When you're ready, schedule daily meetings, ignore any interruptions, and discuss how your relationship is doing. You should try talking more about the present and future than the past if you feel like this is exhausting and just repeating old emotions. You and your partner must often check in to see how you both are doing.

Now is the moment to be cautious and put your relationship first. Moving progress is difficult if there is poor communication. Instead of using "you" words that come out as more accusatory, such as "You never give me any attention after you get home from work," work on using "I" statements to describe your emotions, such as "I feel sad when you don't greet me after you return home from work."

Maintain control:

He could believe that he can dictate to you when and where to see him, but it's up to

you to convince him that you have alternative plans. He sometimes gets to decide when and where to hang out, but you do too. He can hang out whenever it's most convenient for you; you don't have to hang out around his schedule either. Maintaining control over the situation will convince him that you are a serious contender.
He won't be as interested in you if he feels like he controls you.

Chapter 5
Getting it right

Make the decision that is best for you, no magazine, friend, relative, or doctor can advise you otherwise. Your choice becomes considerably more difficult if children are involved. Even though you might believe there is only one correct response, you must ultimately be honest with yourself and listen to what your heart is saying. Finding the truth may take some time, but the most crucial thing is to understand that no one, especially not your partner, has the right to direct your actions or your emotions. However, you should pay attention if your instinct is already telling you what to do.

Decide to be forgiving:
Keep in mind that choosing to forgive someone is truly a choice; it is not something that happens freely without contemplation. You must firmly decide to forgive your partner if you're willing to do so or even if you're just willing to attempt. Though he must put forth an effort to earn your forgiveness because it won't just happen. Accepting that you'll strive to make things work is the first step.
Tell your lover the truth about how you feel. Tell him that you're truly hoping to make things work.

Spend time with each other without discussing the affair he had. Spend quality time with your lover that has nothing to do with the fact that your partner strayed if you want to start mending your relationship. Work on doing the activities you used to enjoy doing together and avoiding the locations that bring up past infidelity.

Before moving too quickly, try to start from the ground up and make sure your connection has a strong foundation through regular interactions.
You can even find a new activity you can enjoy together, like hiking or cooking. You may have a fresh perspective on your relationship as a result.

Look after yourself:
You could feel that taking care of yourself comes last in the face of a dishonest partner. You might not have time to consider things like eating three meals a day, getting some sunshine, or making sure you get enough sleep since you may be experiencing

complex emotions. But you must take good care of yourself if you want to persevere through the trying time and have the strength to work on your relationship.

The following points should be remembered:

Sleep for at least 7-8 hours every night

Work to consume three nutritious meals per day: Although stress may make you more likely to eat unhealthier meals like sugary snacks, you should make an effort to maintain your health to keep your spirits high. Eating fatty foods may make you feel lethargic.

Try to exercise for at least 30 minutes every day:
This is beneficial for your body and mind, it can also allow you some time to be by yourself and forget about the affair.

Keep a journal and make an effort to write in it at least a couple of times per week to give yourself some space to process your thoughts.

Avoid being alone with yourself:
To feel more balanced, spend more time with your friends and family.

Consult a counselor:
Even while not everyone can benefit from counseling, you and your partner should give it a shot if you're attempting to patch things up. The greatest approach to establishing a safe environment for you and your partner so that you can truly feel comfortable sharing your thoughts is by doing this. You may feel like it will be too embarrassing or too much for you, but it may be the best option. Find a therapist you

can depend on, and give your sessions your best.

You should let your partner know that you must go if this is vital to you. Your partner ought to be able to help you out since he betrayed your trust.

Realize when it's over:
It might be time to leave the relationship if you've tried everything to make it work but still can't picture yourself forgiving your partner or moving on. Even though your partner has worked hard to earn back your trust, certain things are just beyond forgiveness. Don't be frustrated with yourself for being unable to forgive your partner. It's time to decide to end the relationship and move on if you find that you are unable to do so despite your best efforts to make it work.

If you believe that you are unable to forgive, try not to be angry or disappointed with yourself. Your partner is the one who initially betrayed your trust, even though you made the effort.
You shouldn't feel embarrassed about yourself for "caving in" if you have managed to move on. Nobody should criticize you for making the decision you believe is best for your relationship.

www.ingramcontent.com/pod-product-compliance
Lightning Source LLC
LaVergne TN
LVHW052114160826
845678LV00015B/3538

* 9 7 9 8 3 5 2 2 3 0 0 6 0 *